My First Team

T-BALL

by KIM THOMPSON

TABLE OF CONTENTS

A Pelican Book

SEAHORSE PUBLISHING

Teaching Tips for Caregivers and Teachers:

Research shows that one of the best ways for students to learn a new topic is to read about it.

Before Reading

- Read the title and predict what the book will be about.
- Read the "Words to Know" and discuss the meaning of each word.
- Read the back cover to see what the book is about.

During Reading

- When a student gets to a word that is unknown, ask them to look at the rest of the sentence to find clues to help with the meaning of the unknown word.
- Motivate students with praise and encouragement.

After Reading

- Discuss the main idea of the book.
- Ask students to give one detail that they learned in the book.

SIGHT WORDS

a	make	to
are	play	we
fly	run	with
it	the	

WORDS TO KNOW

baseball

bat

catch

T-ball

team

We play **T-ball**.

T-ball

baseball

We play with a **baseball**.

We **catch** the baseball.

catch

We **bat** the baseball to make it fly.

bat

We run!

We are a T-ball **team**!

team

Index

Written by: Kim Thompson
Design by: Jen Bowers
Series Development: James Earley

Photos: cover and p.15 ©2015 Joseph Sohm/Shutterstock; p.4 ©2019 Jon Osumi/Shutterstock, ©2018 Jonathan Novack/Shutterstock; p.5 ©2007 Karen Givens/Shutterstock; p.6 ©2013 Rob Hainer/Shutterstock; p.7 ©2017 fs24/Shutterstock, ©2012 Dan Thornberg/Shutterstock; p.8 ©2009 sonya etchison/Shutterstock, ©2006 Stacy Nazelrod/Shutterstock; p.9 ©2014 JenJ_Payless/Shutterstock; p.10 ©2016 Jonathan Novack/Shutterstock, ©2020 Jsita/Shutterstock; p.11 ©2014 Rob Hainer/Shutterstock; p.12 ©2017 Tony-Gibson/Shutterstock, ©2019 Jonathan Novack/Shutterstock; p.13 ©2010 Brian Eichhorn/Shutterstock

Library of Congress PCN Data
T-Ball / Kim Thompson
My First Team
ISBN 978-1-63897-419-2 (hard cover)
ISBN 978-1-63897-534-2 (paperback)
ISBN 978-1-63897-649-3 (EPUB)
ISBN 978-1-63897-764-3 (eBook)
Library of Congress Control Number: 2021953282

Printed in the United States of America.

Seahorse Publishing Company
www.seahorsepub.com

Published in the United States
Seahorse Publishing
PO Box 771325
Coral Springs, FL 33077

SEAHORSE PUBLISHING